THE ECSTASY OF LOVE

PART – 2

NARENDRA KUMAR V
Dr A.C.V.RAMAKUMAR

CONTENT

INTRODUCTION

Love it is a word we all use but strangely we are so confused about it. We think of love as sentiment, as attachment and/or as a kind of lust. Of course we do not say it like this.

The sentiment is the cover for dependence. That leads to attachment that is a kind of clinging. And our love making becomes lust.

Alas!! True love is NOT these things!! It is exactly the opposite if the above three.

There is trust me NO dependence in love and hence no attachment.

Then what is there?

We know it when we meet and SEE our soul mate. That person exists. We see that in part even in friendship that is deep. But here it is in part. Not full enough. We must feel love!!

Get a sense of love!! Get evidence of love.

These writings will give you FULL feeling, sense and truth and even simplicity if love!! We show openly even daringly the feeling of love that might give you that feeling of – es!! yes!!

Read this book and enjoy it!!

Forget your existing notions of love. Bring back your deep innocence.

And REDISCOVER love!!

Wish you love and that physical love that is and should be ECSTASY!!

Ecstasy is connection to your lover!! It is BOTH mind and body.

To find something you must feel it. Then you WILL find it!!

THE ECSTASY OF LOVE

PART - 1

CONCLUSION

LOVE NEVER DIES.

LOVE CANNOT DIE.

LOVE IS YOU.

LOVE IS LIFE.

LOVE IS THE FULL TRUTH!!

A WILD LOVE STORY

I was in love with this girl and everybody told me she was not right for me. She was wild, but I loved her, because she was not obedient, normal, well behaved or even very loyal. I could see in her that she loved each person deeply and separately and that is how I too loved. She was the wild person which I had hidden in me for years.

When we first met, she melted away my defenses which anyway were only on the surface. She laughed at my shyness, and slowly brought me out. But she was serious too, had a wonderful, delicate and sensitive mind. We used to read together, and I could see her eyes, they used to be filled with such intense appreciation of the beauty of words, I could see her naked soul at that moment, and I used to be filled with such maddening desire, such dirty thoughts, that I used to become numb.

She was perfect-for me.

And then I began hearing stories and they seemed impossible to her, her multiple affairs, her free for all attitude as people called her. I did not believe that, and slowly as time passed, one day, I suddenly realized that she was "free for all" and I realized that when I realized that I too was "free for all"...She was me you see, bewitching, no holds barred, innocent, too intense, and too deep not to see deeper than what people saw. So she was admired privately in the aloneness of each person she touched but socially accused.

When I indirectly brought up the topic in our endless conversations, I could see the sadness in her eyes, she lived with a deep sadness, and that moment I wanted to protect her, not knowing in what way, and I felt desperate, and felt a danger that I could not define.

At last It became clear, she was mad about me, she began to become weak, in her love for me, she needed me, and I needed her, and the moment of our ecstatic union was something like an explosion, because in that moment, I and she too realised our uniqueness separately and also , at once , that we were one and the same. We were soul mates.

Strange moment it was, we were in the garden, at night, not a soul around, not a sound, only our breathing, heavy and desperate, our love making, that took us to a pleasure that we did not know belonged to the body or mind or what...we were close to death, death to all barriers, and our bodies answering clearing our doubts, screaming and laughing, wildly like animals, and discovering that life is pure, good, and we were angels then, in a heaven no one had talked about and no none knew of.

Finally we lay, the aftermath a strange peace, so deep and so peaceful, our bodies intertwined and our hands a lock. We lay, talking and we finally drifted off to sleep until the morning , naked light threw its sunshine on our naked bodies. We woke up, smiled and we both knew that the worst and the best was over. and a new life had begun and. that our marriage had indeed been made in heaven when we were born as what we were...

I SEE HER

I see her. Plain she is. Pale.
And then when I talk to her.
She is normal and happy.
And I am so happy.
We eat together, the food she makes.
And we talk of nothing...everything.
Time stops still. And exchanges happen.
One person speaking to another.
Nothing more or less.
And we are like children. Lost. Happy.
Not conscious. Not special. Just we two.
And then we part.
After a long, long time.
And then I go home.
And I realize.
She is in me.
I am in love. I and she. One.
Yet I am I.
And she is she.

The WONDER OF SIMPLE
DEEP, FINAL, LOVE!!

LOVE

I see you, and feel the thing within,
I know you and can understand your every move,
I am quiet, struck,
I need you, now always,
You fulfill me like no other,
You are that special thing i can see
I talk to you and the undercurrent exists
Vibrant, enticing
Taking me into wild imagination,
We touch finally knowing the inevitable
We fall deep in love,
Shocking, rapturous, filled with joy
That wipes out the world
We go on and on exploring the
Limits of ecstasy months pass by
And life has become a great blessing

We are gone forever, fresh is life,
Everyday new, every day an extreme pleasure,
Serene, violent calm, deeply happy and
Finally the cup is filled and life is infinite...

FIND YOUR SOUL MATE....WORTH IT!!

A soul mate friend is simply who gets you with little talking, and thus gives you what you need exactly,

A soul mate friend is also one who pushes you, because he simply sees what you can do, and tells you to do it and insistently,

A soul mate friend loves you, simply because he sees you fully, and laughs at you too when you say something which in bad moods is untrue about you,
He keeps you YOU!

A SOUL MATE FRIEND IS ONE WHO MAKES; LIFE FAR EASIER THAN ALONE,

And a soul mate friend shares all about himself too with you, and it is a kind of double life, more exciting and interesting,
A soul mate friend is like breath, you don't notice him, but you cannot do without him, and this is revealed off and on, in emergency situations,

When you are ready to give, at an instant, ALL for him, you do everything for a soul mate friend,

And I am blessed with my soul mate friends that at times I feel all the great novels and stories are wasted on me!

I am living and seeing, both, so many stories and fairy tales, scripted and enacted in front of me, in life.

Life can be FAR STRANGER THAN FICTION= the highest medium of art!!

TO ALL TRUE LOVERS OF THE WORLD! MY LOVE

You are my strength, my ideal, my highest possible
No, not in the things you say or believe primarily,
But in the way you are, rock solid, strong, bearing me, loving me,
And wanting me and needing me
That fills me with the most unbearable ecstasy
Your deep eyes probe and know without knowing and React
and hold me and kiss me and love me
With a burning passion that brings the man in me to the surface
And we go into another world, my sweetheart,
A world of utter, pure, limitless joy,
We explore, the limits of love in our physical beings
And sweating, and screaming, and bursting out into
Freedom and discovery, a shocking discovery
Of life and its beauty, its fullness, its madness,
And yet, I cannot get enough of you my darling, as
You are the infinitude and embodiment of full life,
I am me with you and to hold you is to find me
And then I do not know where you begin and I end!!
I love you and I can say that a million times,
And yet I cannot be tired and it will not suffice
YOU are LIFE and LIVING, The meaning and glory!!!
Happy Valentine to you and no death would come to our love
It is now and also ever and ever and ever!!!

THE POWER WITHIN

She had been married for 2 years. She lived in a village. Her name was Leela. Her husband was a cook in a hotel in the city. Her husband was that ordinary Indian, and he did not respect her at all. He would often shout at her, and in the initial days of her marriage, when she raised her voice a bit , he thrashed her. She could not protest. Slowly she knew how to submit.

One day, she was in the market, and she noticed that a man was watching her. He looked at her in a strange way, as if he was attracted to her. She found him strange. He was well built and looked like a carpenter, or workman.

The next day she came, and he was there. This time he followed her from a distance, and she looked back at him, her heart pounding, guilty and full of pleasure.

That night, her husband came drunk, as he did usually, and he complained about the food. She stared at him, and he got so angry, that he took the broom, and beat her.

That night she sat outside looking at the stars, after her husband had taken her, in that cheap way, that too had become a routine to her.

She felt lonely, and a deep longing filled her. It surprised her. Next day, she went to the market, and he was there, that man. Today he was dressed very smartly, in tight jeans and t-shirt. her breath stopped.

She walked away, and he followed. Finally she took a dry road that led to the fields nearby, turned and smiled at him, slightly. She could see the look of joy in his face.

Finally she came to a deserted spot, and she went behind some trees and waited. He came.

She asked--why do you look at me like that?

He answered- you are so beautiful..

Do not lie. I am not. What do you want?

Nothing... nothing. Sorry…. and he began to turn back, feeling very guilty.

She felt a pity for him, and a sinking in her heart...

Wait, She said

If you are brave, speak your mind.

He said simply--I want you...I like you..Something about you, you are so so..And then he looked at her...and saw into her eyes...

She stepped forward, and on an impulse, desire burning within her, she let her saree fall. He looked at her with a strange awe.. and then he held her, kissed her.. Violently.. he started moving all over her body, with his lips, and she moaned..they went down together...

That night her husband came. Again drunk. Where is the food? He demanded.

I did not prepare.--she answered.

For a moment he was shocked. She was holding a rod in her hand, a thin rod.

As he came near, she started beating him, on and on went that thrashing, bruising him. He screamed, and ran away from the house..

She stood there and laughed.. Hysterically. All was quiet. She stood there, realizing this was not her home. She did not know that man too, but a strange fearlessness and recklessness took hold over her. She walked out...

She walked an walked...in the dark...as if she could walk for ever. She knew her mother would be angry, but her father would help her. But she felt so happy, free....

HOW ROMANTIC LOVE WORKS

Romantic love is a profound thing, the deepest, the fullest one can feel.
It is an electric thing – passionate, trembling and infinite.
What is that infinitude? Why is that infinitude?
Life is a process of acquiring fundamental values of character to enable us fully and joyously to act out our plan of life.

Life is purposive. Purpose is central to a man's or a woman's character. Purpose is that choice, fundamental choice that rules a man, drives a man, fulfills a man essentially psychologically but also physically (in that he earns his living by that)

A central purpose gives meaning to man's life, integrates his life, is synonymous with life.

A purposeless life is not life and is as close to death as a man can come.

What is involved in a life of purpose? Purpose is a passion that is a profound grounding, an exultant security, for a man. It defines him, so to speak, and provides a wholeness and long range activity to him.

In that sense, it is purpose that makes him take birth as man. Once a purpose is deeply felt, and committed to, man is free! There is no other thought then, no drifting, no running and no pursuit of blind, mindless values....

It is purpose that makes a man rise above the conventional world- the world that runs amok, sightless creatures following rules set by others , with no real passion, a robotism that is swallowing the world, no individuality, hence no character, no ground within the being...

With a purpose, man is free, detached from the conventional world. Yet it is he who creates, preserves, gives meaning to the world.

Purpose is hence naturally, obviously joyous because a man with a purpose has roots, deep roots to live on earth.

It is purpose that gives courage, energy, enthusiasm...
A man of purpose, a man who has essentially defined his identity, given complete meaning to life in thought and action is a passionate man.

He has a tremendous feeling for life. When such a man meets another with the same kind of deep grounding in a great purpose, the result is electric, passionate, trembling, filled with an infinite, deep ecstasy?

Why is it so?
It is a confirmation not in his mind but in front of him, objectified.

It is as if by some miracle, he can touch his purpose, touch his life, feel life by touch, sight, by his senses. It is as if a being comes and says- I am you, see me, hold me to feel yourself. You are hidden but I have brought the hidden in you out as I embody you.

You see, we live in our minds but reality is not in the mind but out there. A purpose satisfies one but we also need to, if such a miracle could be wrought, SEE the meaning of our purpose. Another human being has got the power to give us that on various levels.

Just to see the same purpose in another brings out the deepest confirmation without thought, filling us with a single, overwhelming feeling- ROMANTIC LOVE.

It is an intimacy, the "I" that we are finding a way by which it can see feel, touch, not another physical body but a concrete form and vision of his deepest grounding and foundation.

It is really a simple feeling- deep, infinite, serene and yet violent, tense, trembling. It is a union of thought and sense.

Sex hence is the most intense feeling one can feel. You can while making love, actually find the greatest blessing, because your purpose, your foundation and grounding has acquired more than a sensory value, it has become linked with pleasure.

It is a gift, a natural capacity, inborn, ingrained. To touch, feel and find a pleasure in such a way that one's values are being confirmed. The feeling is – Yes! Yes! Yes!

It is a trembling 'yes' to life, to existence, to the inherent benevolence of being. It is a glorious thing and it is hence, the greatest sin to deny its meaning, its fulfilling potential, its grace, its ecstasy.

A WOMAN'S HUNGER - A HOT POEM!!

Lie, with me, my dear, I need to be laid,
By you, just you, with that
Full, possessing understanding,
Too much, of my deep soul's cravings,
I need to be taken by you with force,
With that utter laughter of your knowledge
Of my need of you, and your needing me,
Like rape, that is what tingles me,
Shakes me with unbearable pleasure,
My MANLY MAN, I need to be hit hard,
Deep and I want to lose the sense of
MIND, BODY, SOUL!! I want to go
Out of this world, experience,
With the stark, naked thrusts,
soft...soft...caressing...
Harder...harder, hard, the highest ecstasy!!
Which only you can give, the
Deepest penetration that can alone
Give me that PEACE and NIRVANA!!!
IT IS POSSIBLE, MINE, REAL
Only with you my Lordly Lord!!,
Come, do it to me... Do it or I will die!!!

A HOT POEM CELEBRATING LIFE...YOU AND I ONE...

Real sex is something that _____
you see that woman, naked, and you SEE her, actually see
through her, and that nudity becomes too much....
that pull in the belly.. And that hot thing rising without, and
deep within you...
you rise and hold your girl..and that touch holds a thing IN
her, and that is a closeness that is incredible, unbelievable,
shocking pleasure..and meaning crazily together!!
Then she is you and you are her, hands, legs intertwine, you
hold her tight to yourself, and that tightness and hardness
says your love so completely, you scream in madness,
and you KISS, the lips, the soft, lips of your girl, and go deep
in the lips, and the feeling...of that sheer woman...makes you a
wild lover...and you kiss, you know how and how much,
you caress, the beautiful hips, and arms and legs, and the
whole body, the caresses are owning that body, and it is an
experience that is that ecstasy that is an answer and such
complete benevolence, such complete wiping off of pain, guilt,
fear...
That it is like a heaven you have reached...you look into her
eyes, and laugh...
Both off you enjoy that caressing and then that upward
movement deep within, suspended in space, stark strokes,
maddening to do and desire reaching the peak of fulfillment..
And then the shocking explosion in the mind, the body,
together!! And you SEE A HEAVEN and you know in that
moment and eternally that life is good, too good, true and
beautiful...
and then you lie for long time, whispering in an intimacy that
has made you both so purely, simply one.. and you sleep......
life is found yet again...

ON SOUL MATES

In life many times, we meet a person and we are attracted without reason, we get this strange, wonderful feeling of intimate, unbearable closeness with the person, we can feel its shape, intangible it is, yet tangible, trembling in intensity and driving us crazy.

This is love and when that happens, we desperately need to CONSCIUOSLY identify that love, the nature of that. That love is your soul mate. People do not know themselves fully, but they do have a nature, a basic nature. They may not have identified that nature, they may cover it up with many things, they may feel opposite to that and act too CONSCIOUSLY.

YOUR NATURE IS YOUR DEEPST FEELINGS, THE DEEPEST WAY YOU LOOK AT THE ORLD BUT IT IS HELD SUBCONSCIOUSLY, YOU HAVE THAT SEMI AWARENES KIND OF FEELING ABOUT IT. The nature of a person is the impression of the person you get not what he says or Even believes but what he deeply is and the living soul within Identified or not. Again it is the conscious -subconscious thing and the drama of that.

All literature is that, all art, all music, what we call flowing and flowering is nothing but the surfacing of the deep nature, the soul if you want to use that word, becoming conscious.

Now when a soul , in this sense meets another, just like that, the subconscious harmonizes, resonates, and that is love, romantic, idiosyncratic, personal, crazy, love , a love without reason, you think, but this is the reason. Now for a man or a woman who knows herself/ himself, it is easy to identify your soul mate, you see and it is love at first sight obviously!!

But is it first sight or is it all your life, as that person is you only.
So you need to in that meeting, and that meeting too will help you,
see yourself in her and know it.
It is a great feeling, probably the greatest because your entire self is involved in the other person.
That is a soul mate, that is real, possible, yours, but you have to know yourself and know your discovery and the miracle of it.
Marriages are made in heaven in that sense.

THE MIND BLOWING WOMAN

She is a serious, an extremely talented person. She loves to explore her field all the time. There is no real still moment for her. even when she relaxes, She likes to have that deep thrill, enjoyment that she is used to, in day to day life!! In that sense, she lives a life of grandeur. Each day, is special, with new ideas, insights, great interactions.... and above all magical moments in work that cannot be computed, expressed or even held.. Demanding expression ....it is a flowing passion, serene, and clear cut that moves her.

All the world is her stage, but she is not the world, and she knows it. But not really fully. She is innocent, at times generous too, because she is disbelieving. The feeling of living in a skewed world, common and natural, is always present.
So she alternates between touching the heights of happiness and at other times, rarely, the depths of sadness.

She is utterly beautiful, open and a fearless face and structure and manner and body language, that is so extremely confident, yet unselfconscious, that shocks people and draws them to her or scares them.
But alas!! There is no person who can even begin to match her talent, and her enormously passionate life....
She is lonely, but she is not negative, she is a matter of fact.. and accepted this fact serenely.

She is a great friend, when she makes one, and then she is fully, irrevocably giving and loving, considerate and understanding...
She is an incredible girl, no , not because she is great, but she is refreshingly simple, human and just another "girl"...full and free...

THE MAGICAL UNION OF SOUL MATES

I SEE HER, MY OTHER, MY MIRROR, a thing exactly like me, in another body, opposite to me yet same. We are given by nature that physical ability and we can't but attract each other!!

When we hold hands, kiss, caress, each other, it becomes a magical union, of soul and body, and it is heavenly and earthy, love and sheer madness to explore the body. Oh! The magnificent body that is soulful and expressive, that gives an extreme pleasure, an ecstasy that IS both of the body and soul. It gives me the joy of sheer living, joy of being, a confirmation, a confidence, a reverence of my utter goodness and power!

It is a HUMAN thing, and in that act and discovery, I discover everything! I understand the simple thing, the magic and the utter simplicity of living, making us laugh and enjoy the whole act in utter innocence and complete unseriousness, carefree, but deeply wise too.

We realize we had earned it long ago, were waiting simply to meet and fulfill that which we had created within us, a profound self made soul that impregnates the beings that we are today!

The mind and the body are ONE, the reverence IS of this earth, the cleansing is all the rot of centuries, Adam and Eve are born again , this time realising that the fruit of knowledge has to be eaten, that it is not a sin at all, it is the greatest celebration, it is the holy thing!

The pleasure wipes out that "sin" and shudder of the extreme evil of evil of hating the good because it is the good, the extreme envy that does not want men and women to live and love...

We go on and on, we reach the pinnacle yet again, happy children we are, basking in the golden light of illuminated knowledge, feeling the beauty, the wonder and the glory of life!!

A STORY OF TRUE LOVE

I FELL IN LOVE WITH HER, I HAD TO. There is no choice left to me. This girl I met ...well...you don't even know that such a woman is and can be. You feel a kind of kinship, the respect you get from her is so true, real...how can I resist it, tell me...

She looks at you, speaks the truth, hurts you, but after a few days you go back because you like the masochism of liking truth, the way she expresses it, only she.

OMG...I am madly in love. I know this is love, admiration, love that is so much but then it is its own justification.

I always felt like an ordinary guy, until I met her. And she did not do anything, but then she looked at me. She does not even know that...she is innocent but obviously not dumb. She is extremely intelligent, but a kind of in love with using her mind, and her feelings are so true.

You also feel tender when you see her, suddenly you feel you need to be a man with her, protect her, but from what you don't clearly know. She is fiercely independent, cannot help be, she loves the truth.

She is like a man-woman and I bet you have never met a type like that, and if you have no matter what pain came into your life, that would have given you LIFE...

YOU KNOW WHAT IS SECURITY, EXACTLY A FRIEND LIKE HER... BECAUSE A KIND OF DOUBLE PROTECTION COMES,

You become better, and she is close at hand, you cannot but be the best with her, because she needs you not.

For the first time you understand love really, directly. You understand there is NO SUCH thing of what people call love!! it is hyped, and how!!

You almost begin to hate that concept. You kind of enter a realm of higher, clearer, simpler love.

She is cold and sweet, she is passionate and tender, she is unlike anything I have ever felt, she is LIFE!!

She has made me happy in life, finally.....I need nothing and nobody now

THE LIMITS OF JOY

I look into you,
Deep, and find myself.
Madness seizes me,
I hold you and tremble
At the sudden knowledge
Of how precious
You are to me,
A value that
Can't be computed
Because it has
Become infinite…
a pleasure that
Has become limitless.
We are locked in
Ecstasy and this
Doubles up my life ,
Gives fuel and reality
a kind of art
a fulfillment
Just because you are
And you exist.
We go on and on,
Touching the limits
Of joy and
Pain, fear, doubt
Wiped out from
the face of the earth…
Serenity and violence
Incredibly one!

MIRROR MAGIC

When you find your other,
You end living in the mind,
You achieve the impossible,
You see yourself, in front of you,
Your deepest self becomes sensorial,
Concretized, a blinding reality.

You need that self now,
Selfishly, deeply, irrevocably,
You feel it as your very own,
The other for you, and you for the other,
A mesmerizing, wondrous, breathless union,
Of two individuals who can't be one,
But are magically and actually!

You are filled with a sense of wonder,
You are deeply fulfilled just to see,
The existence of the other a profound sanction,
And fills you with benevolence and bliss,
With no need to prove anything.

A constant fascination to see the other,
Move, feel, think, express, respond,
The other becomes important to you,
Selfless it feels but actually deeply selfish,
You want the other and it is a gift to you.

You express and express in wonder,
Knowing too well that it is the impossible,
And the value cannot be computed or expressed,
Peaceful you become finally,
Fully living the entity that you are,

You seem to have found the fount of life!

I love you, love you, love you, -
You say a million times,
And yet it seems not enough,
And you find another way,
You hold each other,
Explore the limits of physical pleasure,
That magically becomes an unbearable ecstasy,

You are filled with a fuel to achieve all that you desire,
Your mind seems to have sharpened,
And all power seems to have come to you.

On and on you journey in life,
Everyday special, everyday a celebration,
An utter separation and a total union at once,
As the other is but your MIRROR MAGIC!

You hold the secret, the two of you,
A team you are and now you
Find the strength to take on the whole world!

ECSTATIC UNION

I look at her,
my girl, and
I want to hold her,
Embrace her,
tell her,
by some magic ,
how beautiful and
precious she is.
She is too good,
almost not true,
yet real,
functioning, living.
It seems
like a miracle,
this thing before me.
I kiss her,
hold her,
and a madness
seizes me.
Suddenly I find ,
in the act,
the way to tell her
and a way
to express,
my own deep self,
simultaneously,
miraculously!
I laugh, in
astonishment,
as always.
I prize it, hold it ,
a precious secret.

She closes her eyes
and we sink deep
into an ecstatic union.
It goes on and on
and we seem
to reach the limit.
I cannot believe it
and then it hits us
and we know
in that moment
what life is-
final, complete,
nothing left
to be desired ever.

INTIMACY

to see a person,
to see, to wait,
and see,
give that space
to unfold
and see...
and to get that person,
from the inside...
and by seeing
you are allowing
to be seen,
so letting that be...
hurting ..if it happens,
but holding...
and then
THAT CLICK!!
You get CLOSE!!!
INTIMATE...
tied.. loved....
yet separate..
Wondrously ONE too

WHEN WILL LIFE , IN THAT HIGHEST SENSE EVER
BEGIN, LIFE THAT BEATS IN THOSE RARE HEARTS WHO
KNOW LIVING,THINKING AND LOVING....???

SIGH!!!

I Saw Deep Into Her Eyes...
And lo, I lost my sense of self
Another self took its place..
hey who are you?
I cried..but it was me.
I vanished, and ....
The eyes locked.
And then the lips, the body,
and the oneness so simple
A laughter released,
A steely, rough laughter!!
Violent, silent, deep, and calm
The trance, the ecstasy.
Final..
On and on, the moans
The kisses, the caresses.
And finally the beats
and the rhythm
of the pounding it,
The unbelievable magic.
Of two who had shared
that utter sense of life!!
as worship and utter joy!!
Finished. Realized. Joy forever.

PRESSURE ---

It is a nice one,
when you do that...
it is needed, desired...
wanted, loved...
do it with that love pressure...
do it with that real touch..
and do it not just
WITH SLAPS
but every single thing,
that would make her
want more of that..
more and more...
screaming,
agonizing pleasure...
then do it with all kinds
of pressures...
pressure is lovely...
it is a communication- direct ..
it is an expression
of your passion,
and finally when the
limit of thrust is given,
then she should know
that you are giving it to HER..
that is magic...
and the pleasure turns
MAGICALLY, WONDROUSLY
to something most people
do NOT experience or know..
mate the mind..
and then pressure her...
all the way....
TO HER SCREAMING, LOVING limit!!

THE STORY OF LISA

Every person has a story and Lisa is no exception.

Lisa was a hard nut from childhood. She has a strange and somewhat rare quality of rationality, rare in a woman.

That makes her a hard hearted (to this world) person outside but warm, loving, soft inside.

She grew up and, as is usual, in this world, nobody tells you and communicates how to give shape, meaning and full reality to your life, to your deepest nature, Lisa grew up averagely with a modest development of applicative, released intelligence.

Thus the only value she found was love – in Sastri. Thus came, in this one issue, her really, deep fiery nature.

She perceived in Sastri a strong, happy, sincere man and she loved.

In India, that led to an elopement as Sastri, is a Hindu and she is a Christian.

She was clear and simple about her choice and that reflects her deeply loving, nature intelligence and goodness.

Well, they married and Sastri was sincere but aimless, doing good to all because that's all and how he would express his sincerity to all, he was also ambitious but not in the hardworking sense. He placed a high importance on money, an exclusive importance and that undercuts his character and limits him though he is sincere, deeply within.

The two are happy and fate had something else in store for Lisa. She could not remain passive.

The demands of life were on her. She worked hard and she has that solid realism and learnt some applications in computers and did a job for 7 years.

Later with the help of benefactor she set up a small net center.

Sastri, because of his contempt for hard work of a small kind, always opposed Lisa's desire to learn. But again, she rebelled and learnt, first the application of computers, but later did her MSC in computers.

Again, there was, as usual, nobody to guide her. She learnt nothing in MSC but her quest did not stop. She has joined a good course in further application in computers and somewhere within her she wants to learn and grow.

We see this young girl, alone in the world fighting but blindly, with only her native, intelligence and deeply loving nature to guide her.

She has found a partial satisfaction in her husband and in her work / learning.

But she is a human being and the soul needs ascent, light.

What must be her deepest thoughts, her dreams, her desires, her wishes, her pain, her happiness?

She is ambitious, not dead, fighting, not even knowing that hers is a fight.

Wisdom she needs but where is it?

She must be feely a strange unfulfillment that she can't voice, can't give words to, hence unable to grow faster.

She can only struggle. She will find her path, it will take time, because the soul pushes on for fulfillment like a plant that goes towards the light.

LOVE ON A TRAIN...

The train moved on and Raj looked at the girl, yet again. He laughed, soundlessly inside. This girl was such an actor!! There she sat, and she acted coy, soft, and simple, and obedient. But she was not. He could guess it.

Her husband was sitting beside her dozing off, he looked tired after the ordeal that is a wedding. She had just got married.

Why do these people marry at all. This farce, he thought idly... Then he turned his head and looked at the lovely earth, having forgotten the wedding party and their frivolous conversation. He was an artist and a professional photographer, and he took in that sights that moved past him.

It was finally night, and everyone got ready to sleep having finished their dinner.

Raj too stretched himself, and closed his eyes, and went to sleep at an instant.

He woke up, at around 3-30. He could not sleep for too long, though he was a good sleeper.

He decided to walk to the end of the compartment and look at the night from the door.

he walked the length of the compartment, and stood by the door.

As he stood, he noticed that he was not alone. At the other door, the girl was there.

She looked at him, and he suddenly saw her real self. She was smart, intelligent and perceptive. there was faint smile in her eyes. He knew she was that type that is stuck, in India, that wants to break free and cannot, that is average minded but nice inside, and with desires , soon to die, as she was married.

Suddenly he got this wild idea to give her a smoke..

Would you like to try? He asked. Handing out his pack.

"I do smoke" she said, with gratitude, and took a cigarette, and lit it taking his lighter.

He was shocked to see that she was an expert, the way she inhaled, and the way she let out with her eyes closed...

AAHH!! Feels so good, she said, and that sentence meant more than the cigarette alone...

The train moved on....they glanced at each other from time to time.

He observed her now more closely. She was pretty, but dark and dusky, she had a sharp nose, but very thin lips, that gave her a touch of manliness that was very cute. She was very thin, and yet she looked very strong.

She finally finished her cigarette. Raj looked out, and stood there enjoying the sights.

Then suddenly he felt someone was standing beside him. It was that girl.

He made room for her. They stood looking and yet stood feeling each others prescience close. It was nice, as it is usually, when there is meaningful silence. The train moved on....

Raj felt her person now, he could feel her breathing that came in gasps and he could also feel as if he could hear her heartbeat. And it was erratic, and excited.

He turned and looked into her eyes, and the eyes did not flinch, they looked into his. For a long time, they looked cool, calm at each other....it was comforting, and soothing. Raj let her be, let himself be, did not question all this by anything, let there be no judgment.

They stood looking at each other, and in that glance, they knew each other in that wordless sense in which simply anybody could know anybody.

Now they held each other and stood side by side, and were also careful that they would not be seen, but Raj took care of that, by a side standing.

They stood there. And both felt one and so happy....

Happiness is a lovely thing. It wipes out thought, doubt.

Finally they moved in to the washroom, and inside they laughed, and they kissed and they made love, simply and with abandon, but not taking too much time.

Then they lay in each other's arms, and she said---thank you...

YOU GAVE ME the courage to give up...this is my first night, and tomorrow, I will file for divorce.

Raj said---I...

But she stopped him..no It was nice to know you..I know more that I cannot say, about you. You are something...she let the sentence hang, and walked out silently, with a last smile....

The train moved on....

FREEDOM THAT IS LOVE!!

I COULD FEEL his freedom, within, feel it bad, that space I felt OMG!! It was more than love, it was freedom, complete..

It was a kind of service, yet I could feel the utter selfishness in him, is this that pull we call love, I wondered, but all I wanted was him to take me, right there, right then...

We had to fall in love..And rise in life from then on, armed with our union yet separation...

He gave me freedom..Himself too....

AGAIN ONE - IN ANOTHER

He kissed her on the lips,
And he was struck by a vision
Suddenly of that whole self of hers,
Her soul, and reflected in her body.
Her soul became her body now..
And an instrument of sheer pleasure,
Her held her tight, explored her
First violently, he wanted to know her
Through her every part,
And he could know her, and her response too!!
It was LOVE MAKING-literal!!
THEY LAUGHED, THEY MOANED,
Two innocent beings who knew nothing
except simple plain truth of love!!
And then the ascent began.
He did not believe this happening
Yet it was that blessed thing again!!
ON AND ON HE REACHED DEEP INTO HER
BOTH EXPRESSING HOW MUCH THEY WERE ONE
IT WAS LIKE HER BODY WAS A MAGIC MIRROR,
AND HIS CARRESS COULD HOLD HER PERSON
AND GIVE HIM THE REFLECTION
THROUGH PLEASURE
YES!! YES!! YES!!
THEY SAID , YET AGAIN..
TO THE BEAUTY AND WONDER,
THE SHEER BENEVOLENCE OF LOVE!!
AND FINALLY reached the peak of ecstasy!

THAT CONNECTS... (A STORY)

I met Manoja that day. It is now almost 15 years, but I still remember that day. I had gone to the church, with a friend on Sunday, he was singing for the first time, and he wanted me to be there, as support. I am an atheist, and have always been, but I loved my friend, and he was a strong believer in Christ, and love...and I rather liked him, he was so innocent, pure in his own silent way...

I sat at the front, and he began to sing, and he sang well, and with feeling. I like these church songs sometimes, and they connect to me, they talk about being good, and this song talked about being good to oneself, and thankfulness, a feeling I share...though not in a religious way, but as intensely.

It was then that I saw her...she was standing at a corner talking to someone, and she wore, a short shirt, and a white skirt, that hung around her, beautifully.

No one would call her beautiful, but she was and in fact she had that face that I cannot miss, hard, and full of that glow that comes from sensitivity and intelligence.

I asked my friend later who she was, and he took me and introduced me. I found that she was the teacher of Bible there, and she also counseled. I joked with her that I needed counseling and that I was not a Christian.

And then she said- In that sense, even I am not.

What do you mean? - I asked.

And then she explained that she simply felt and sensed the truth in Jesus, and his words.

She took a great liking for me, in the sense that she wanted to meet me again, so we agreed. I too was curious to know this girl...

We met, and in 2 weeks and after many discussions it all became clear...since then I have become so wise.

She told me, that being human was what Jesus had taught. And when I asked her, how God and human could be reconciled, she said that there is that universal spirit. And each of us is a part of that.

I said I believed in only man, only what I sensed, and she began looking at me tenderly, and with pity, as if I was doomed, I found that crazy, and told her.

It took, time, and I knew where this would end, and what she would accuse me of...it was nerve racking for her too, because at times she seemed to feel so close to me (and it was true also), so connected and I was really painfully in love with this crazy girl, who would anyway break with me, and I felt at least she sensed true love from me, unmistakably.

In lonely moments with no "universal love", she would remember my selfish love.. and yes, she finally had the last word---

She said, that I was in love only with myself, and that I was selfish, and that she would pray for me, and I told her, that I cannot even pray, but I can love...

Somewhere is that beautiful girl, lost in a loveless world, seeking refuge in god, unable to face this brutal world....but GOD bless her, and I mean it....

A LIFE SAVED --- A STORY

K climbed up the long walk up. She was terribly depressed and was in a dark mood. But there was no reason in that mood. She was tired. She had been fired yet again from her job, because she had fought for her ideas that were really good, but nobody was there to listen to her. She was a writer of cinema scripts and she had joined a production company due to her talent at a very young age. But precisely because of that she had to leave...

She did not want to think about it. She simply wanted to be alone on her favorite hill, in the evening and no body came in that spot. It overlooked the sea and you could see the waves going so slow and relentlessly from that height. It was an undiscovered spot.

At last she reached her spot and found that somebody was there under the very tree which she felt was hers...

But she suddenly she heard a song..a humming coming from there. It was a man sitting there and singing.

She was struck by the way he sang. He was humming crazily. He was deeply immersed in singing and had come there to sing alone. Not wanting to disturb him, K sat there at a distance hiding behind another tree and listened...

The notes moved...they did not feel like notes but were moving with a feeling and statement that had become obvious to the singer..so that he was simply enjoying, actually laughing through his music!!

He looked as if he was playing a game with his own ability, his own self!! The notes surprised one at each moment and it was very deep but also very light!! The notes and the SONG moved on and on and it was shocking how much could be conveyed by just humming with no instruments....

Time passed...minutes..and one full hour...
K sat there transfixed at this man who made life so simple, and happy!! She simply wanted to get up and throw herself to the winds and DANCE her heart out!! The SONG was so full of light hearted energy!!

Suddenly the song reached its end and a deep silence pregnant with meaning filled the place. Both sat there and she could feel him just with that silence.....after a long time, it began to be dark...the man got up..

K got up suddenly. He moved off and she could see his face...a chiseled face, full of beauty, and flaming joy...she fell in love with him, a love at first sight, a love that wanted nothing, a love that was justification itself....and she was filled with deliverance....

Thank you--my friend, she whispered as he moved away...

A STORY - SMILE AGAIN

The train moved on and I looked at her for the hundredth time. She looked so sad, and it pained me because she was strong and it is the saddest thing to see a woman, a strong woman and sad. I felt bad.

She was beautiful, but she was pale and colorless. And that gave an impression of feelings that were held very deep. And thus she had the beauty of cold sculpture. She was fair, and had a broad forehead, and very sharp nose and full lips with her lower lip opened up a little as if a thought had stopped.
The train moved on. The sound of the train had a lovely rhythm, and it gave a soothing feeling to a progression that would not stop. I began to have crazy feelings looking at her. She looked older to me by around 5 years and she would be 30, I thought.

On and on went the train and she was looking at the earth, and I was sitting opposite and she had not turned her face. She sat like a statue. She was like that when I had entered.
The compartment was occupied but it was not rushed. The same passengers. An older man sat beside her, he looked like her father. Beside him was an old woman dozing with her dropped?

Beside me near the window and opposite to her was a woman, in her 40s and she was listening to music. There was no one beside me.

The side 2 sea tar too was free.

We were all going to Delhi and I had taken a train to see all the sights that I used to see long back as a child when we used to travel from Vijayawada to Delhi.

I was going for my job, as a visual designer in a top ad agency. I wanted to see India and the journey was very good.

But I was drawn to that girl opposite me.

Suddenly she turned and our eyes had to meet as I had been looking at her only without anyone realizing it, she was in my field of vision.

And that first look was strange. Her eyes moved a bit and as if she had registered something. Then she got up and walked down to the wash room.

And then it hit me. Her structure, the way she walked down to the length of that train, made me realize that she was close to my kind of a woman. She was confident, straight forward and very attractive. Her gait had the strong, confident steps that marked her to be a person who wanted to have life in her hands…and the way her open pony tail moved was incredible, it seemed to signify a joyous nature.

After sometime I saw her again coming back. I averted my gaze towards the window.

She was back to her window.

And then I realized, I don't know how, she wanted to see me. It was an instinct, by the way now she would look away from the window. I let her see me by NOT looking at her and I could feel myself being scanned!!

She was very perceptive..

An hour passed and 2…and 3….soon, it was evening…. The train moved and by now we had felt close enough.

It was night and we all had slept. I could not sleep but finally at 1 I dozed off.

Then suddenly my eyes opened...It was 4 AM I could hear distinctly sobs. The sounds were very faint but I am abnormally sensitive. I was not sure. She was sleeping below my birth. I sat up. And strained my sharp ears. Indeed she was sobbing. It sounded too loud to me but no one was hearing.

It was morning, the train was racing now..and I love trains and the earth that sped past. I was sitting in the unoccupied 2 sea tars and she was still sleeping, the woman in her forties had got up and we chatted for a while.

Then finally at around 7 she got up, the lonely woman. I had named her that in my mind.

She got up, and I was sitting opposite and she glanced and I don't know why but I felt kind of close to her and smiled a bit with my lips fully with my eyes. We had had no conversation. She went to the wash room and came back. She had a drained look, the sad, infinitely sad look was all over her f ace. And I could almost see all that nakedly.

This time I decided to get a conversation started. We still had a whole day, almost 14 hours to go.

We managed to strike a conversation. I found that she was alone, unmarried and she was travelling with her dad, and she had taken him to a retreat in the south for an alternative treatment and she too needed a retreat.

Then for a long time we were silent. I got up and went up to the door. I like standing for long hours at the door. I stood there as the train rhythmically sped past.

She came. I did not notice when she did. But she was there standing beside me. I was shocked but like warmed too to see her confidence and trust in me.. But she was attractively reserved too.

"Wanted to spend some time talking to you...feel like ...you look very different."

I liked that..."in what way do you mean. I am different. But.." "You see, we live in this world and we expect so much, and we love and desire and want. But you know what? We get nothing. It is so perfectly cruel, this world. But then, simultaneously it is not like that at all. I mean it is kind of mixed...see the earth, and the wind blowing now, and we two talking..it is nice...there are nice people...but..."

The words hit me. This was me. I had always carried this pain for ages since childhood, the feeling of being an outsider...the feeling sometimes that one should go, just leave and go away from earth...and mostly a pain that has no solution..

I don't know why... suddenly I broke down...flashes of her sad face, my past hurts...her sobbing... love losses... pain so extreme you did not know whether you would survive...and now this girl who had unashamedly come to me with something she saw...I felt such pity, and compassion truly....

I started sobbing. ...and said...sorry ...between chokes...luckily there was nobody...and the sink was beside...I went up...and washed my face...and when I looked up...I saw one of the serenest and happiest faces I had ever seen...she simply hugged me there and then, and kissed me on the cheek and said, "Thank you"

And this is the way, Shanti and I became the best of friends and her world and mine were one....

One look, one true understanding can save a life, a life that should be saved…life is precious as hell….dear friends…take care….

A SHORT STORY…THE DIVORCE

Sita came out of the courthouse. Her divorce was over and she did not feel like getting into her car. It was evening and not much traffic was there on the roads. She decided to walk.

It felt as if an age was over. She felt strangely free. It was an odd feeling. Because now she was alone, and she had no need to convince, cajole, force, influence , entreat, expect, be hurt, be happy or anything at all. She had found the freedom to just be!!

It was not as if Prashant was wrong or anything. He was still her close one and now a good friend. But she suddenly felt clear in her mind with such a shocking simplicity and happiness, she actually felt guilty. How can I be so happy? She thought in wonder.

Now she could do the things she always had wanted to do. She could sing on with abandon, she could sketch and write being the whole artist that she was.

And she felt the hunger in her to speak, sketch and sing. She had learnt so much and now she felt the joy of wanting to express, the expectant joy!!

Also, she had grown to the limit. She realized that love is alone and that you need to love yourself, consummate your own destiny before the thought of love. She grasped that love is not a pleasure but an add on and now strangely she grasped the beauty and rarity of love.

At the same time, she also grasped how each person had a right to this kind of love…she felt so benevolent at this moment and she stopped and smiled at the world around her. She knew that the new life had already begun…and life was beating in her heart…

THE PROSTITUTE

Once, there was a prostitute. Her name was Sheela. She was pretty, she was born to extremely poor parents and was pushed into prostitution early in life. Initially, it was unpleasant and t pained her but she hardened herself to it and slowly she got used to it. Then it became a kind of lifestyle and a routine and finally she settled in it and lost all her feelings and became dead inside. She even lost the feeling of loosing something.

At the time of this story, she was in this state, 27, and a professional prostitute.

It was at this time that a strange thing happened to her. She fell in love. The man, or rather the boy, was Puneet.

Puneet was only 18 and one day he had come to the brothel and had selected her.

He looked deep into her and she felt a bit strange at his glance that was so intent.

The thing is – she fell for him because he made her conscious of herself as a woman, as a person, as a soul. He made love to her, to her soul. He reached into her deepest self and made her feel special and with that special glance, gesture and almost artfully, he made love to her – caressed her, kissed her, so tenderly and yet successfully, passionately.

When he left her after the first night, she took his number and she wanted him day & night. He came and she could not charge anything. He was extremely mature for his age and possessed her violently, though 18.

He was not sentimental. Strangely that was the best part. It was pure, hence cold, almost calculated love making and he was an expert.

Days became blissful and meaningful for her. Every night he came.

But suddenly one day, he stopped. He answered her frantic calls and he said he was going to the US to study.

Her heart sank and she went into a deep depression. She could not bear anybody touching her.

One day the head of the brothel, the man running the show forced himself up on her.

And a strange thing happened. She became numb and feeling less. She felt nothing. A strange importance took hold over her.

Nobody came hear her as she was dead body on bed. It surprised her too.

A change had come into her. She once looked into the mirror for a long time; she felt she was beautiful. She felt peaceful, cut off and happy inside, as if she was a value.
She left prostitution. She worked as a nurse in a hospital and she carried Puneet's photo always. She didn't need him too much. It was not sentimental. It was more, much more than that, a fulfillment, something divine within her was wrought just because one man – pure, clean, and passionate had seen her, had possessed her, owned her.

It was a transfusion that made her realize the preciousness of life like Valmiki, she took a leap from utter degradation to the heights of purity. She understood by implication – those who did not know happiness – at a glance she understood that the whole world was steeped in a kind of prostitution – adjusting, covering oneself, dying a silent death, never to be redeemed.
She lived with her precious discovery and helped and lit up lives all around her.

COME TO MY HOME....

you will find here the ecstasy and the agony of LOVE
You will find here the warmth, the beauty and the soulfulness of FRIENDSHIP.
You will find here the joy in LEARNING AND DISCOVERING
you will find here the things that touch the SOUL.
You will find here the means to and the power of having a PURPOSE.
You will find here HAPPINESS.
You will find here what it really means to have KNOWLEDGE
You will find here TRUE STORIES of Great men/events.
You will find here all that you mind, heart/soul hungers for....Come feel the joy of LIVING!!!
You will find here that there can be eyes that truly see, ears that truly hear...

One in Mind, Body and Soul
She stood before me, and let her clothes fall off,
She looked at me, plain and simple, my love,
I looked at her in awe, with a reverent feeling,
There was nothing in me but just looking,
I looked at her, straight, through and through,
No mask existed, nothing existed, just she and me,
I took time and kept looking at her, she smiled
The confident, happy, child like smile of hers,
She was a woman through and through, and I a man
Simple it was and filled me with the deepest pressure and ache,
She came to me and when I kissed her on the lips,
It became beyond both of us, violent and laughing,
The moans began, sweet and filled with shocking pleasure,

We explored each other, freely, full of greedy, violent possession,
Human animals we were, to the extreme, both aching to devour,
And then the ascent, and the penetration deep into the soul
The body, mind vanished, we became vessels of ecstasy,
On and on we went in perfect rhythm and madness!!
And finally the screams the sweat, the hunger , the driving power
Drove us to the limits of joy, breaking all barriers,
Surrendering to each other,
In an intimacy that was so complete, wondrous,
Yet it was real, and that was the incredible,
Out of the ordinary reality and yet deeply rooted to earth!!
When we screamed and the shattering, staggering joy
Entered us and released itself,
When the warmth became fluid, and spirited and no dividing line,
When we fell in love, yet again in a confirmation too divine,
We realized, this is life, Yes!! Yes!! This is it!!!

A FATHER'S WISH

Waiting for the day when
She comes to me and says....
"Dad, I have fallen in love with this thing,
My god, this is what i want to DO
All my life , all the time..."
I have fallen in love with---
The possibility of human POWER- MY POWER!!
I have found the fount of life, and now I get it!!!
My god, so much joy!! So much work!! So much excitement!!
I am in love, dad, I am in love!!! With life!!! "

HOME, SWEET HOME

A home is a haven, a secure place where we can relax. You don't have to pretend, don't have to have that steely hypocrisy that is needed in the world, a world where people are caught up in their shells, caught up with their own empty, pseudo identities, where what is absent is a real, clean, true love.

Home lets you be – your own real, happy, self. It is necessary to have a place like that to wash away the shocks, the strains, the pressures that the real world gives you.

Hours you spend in relaxation but not idly. Your thoughts, ideas, resurge. The passion pours forth – yet again. You get a tremendous strength. You relax in the beauty of living, listen to your piece of music, read your favourite books or just do nothing.

You find your meaning, again and that gives the energy to do a 100 things, again.

MADDENING DESIRE AND ECSTASY!!

The touch, that smooth wondrous skin, and you caress it, and are transported, with a touch of a button, to that erotic zone, and you look deep in her eyes, and you both know the meaning of the act, that dirty act, that is divine, and you both smile..

You possess her, and caress her, she clutches you wildly, moaning and taking it all in.

On and on you go, kissing her, on the lips full and violent, yet softly and delicately, savoring that unbelievable, priceless body, and mind of her, your girl....

Like animals you make, love realizing too well, this is awesome, and too much, too good, and true!!Sheer pleasure that cannot be lived for long...

You feel that sense of being nakedly seen, and THAT drives you mad yet again, and it suddenly becomes the statement of the simple, the grounded, the holiness on earth, chaste and free,

And finally your driving pleasure, hard and real... and on and on you go, and then finally that hit!! When you scream that one word--GOD!!

It is God, the best and the highest in you and in her that you reach, a reverence turned into sheer wondrous pleasure given by nature, making a heaven here and now on earth!!

You lie together, in utter love, that aftermath, and sleep in bliss, with nothing desired ever....

EROTIC ONE ... ME IN YOU AND YOU IN ME

The curve...just that sheer ,
delightful, curve, that smooth skin,
wrapping me with tingling excitement,
huge curve here, but so perfect,
pull it up man, push up and begin
that great inner journey of ecstasy,
deep within the mind, body...
possess your girl, through and through,
hey!! leaving nothing!! deep you go...
caress, kiss...with a breathless excitement
yet again given to you as a gift,
smooth caresses, hard ones
on that smooth thing that is you
in a another wondrous form,
hot stuff, breathless, enveloping you
in LOVE TOO EXTREME,
and laughing in release, in pleasure,
pure and simple...and then the ascent,
inwards, going on and on
and pounding it in, hard, harder,
and finally the peak that is a
screaming union, and a divine ecstasy
filling your whole self...
out of this world,
yet strangely earthy...
and simply YOU!!!

YOU ARE ENOUGH FOR ME

Before I met you, I loved so many people, ..there was a so much hunger in me to fulfill myself and yet I was always left starving.

The people I met were lovely, good people. But life is so harsh that goodness and loveliness are not enough for the hungry soul...

The soul needs something specific, definite and complete. It needs salvation and when it comes, finish!!

Nothing else is needed then and that is what you are to me, no, not a friend, or even a soul mate, but a person that I can like with complete ACCEPTANCE and that solves my need. You have done that. I don't feel like looking or even talking to people anymore. I am back to my lonely shell, doing a million things because I know you are and you exist...

Strange is it not...we don't need a buffet...we need just a square friend.

YOU EXIST FOR ME FINALLY

She blows my mind
with such deep comments
and all simple, obvious ,
that which I had held
in my ;loneliness
in a world which
said everything
except that which was
glaringly simple
She said it also with
conviction, courage and directness.
And I had no choice
but to fall head over heels in love
My loneliness mercifully ended for life.
Thank God, from now
I have yet another one...

THE THING ABOUT MARRIAGES

Marriages are funny. You sometimes hate but deep within you love so much, that your partner is an inseparable almost bodily part of you. Thus the pain of separation, fights is too much. Marriage is a union, of two bodies but actually one soul. So much togetherness, habitually leads to a need for each other that could become infinite. Marriage is holy. The love is there, that need not be told, precisely because it is there. The love is felt as a simple truth and when that is debated, it is hurting.

Strange are marriages. So much joy and sometimes so much pain that feels not like the usual pain but kind of different, personal and deep.

Marriage is an unshakeable trust much beyond any practical miscommunication or problem. Marriage is a point of no return.

Marriage is deep affection, needing and fulfilling acceptance so complete that there is no real tension!!

Marriage is thus, a deep security and happiness. That is why I guess marriages have existed for centuries.

This is the reason marriages actually need space and freedom. Because the prison is already erected, the sweet prison of togetherness. Now with almost that kind of motherly "taken for granted peace", one needs wings to fly.

Marriage maybe is a second childhood, because by nature man needs company and deep security of needing and being needed.

And of course marriage is that beautiful, deep, innocent physical union that has to happen with powerful magnetic attraction, the deep infinite love needs that solace of being held and one in and out for that bliss that can never ever be measured.

Marriages are such a wonder, two human beings so close, yet apart, pressure to be one and with each other, yet needing and wanting freedom, both co existing, and the subtle adjustments and harmonious dance carried out from experiencing each other , inside and outside....

MARRIAGE

Marriages are made in heaven
I look at her (my wife)
and I realize that
I need to prove nothing.
She is more than mine,
she is me.

She tells me often
that she can't say 'I love you'.
How can I say 'I love you'
to myself she protests
and it is true.

She is sweet, too sweet.
My doubts, loneliness, fear
dissolves in her simple love.
I smile at the simplicity
in wonder, in pure happiness.

A God must exist
I sometimes feel
for the serendipitous event
of bringing us together
and making us one in life.

One day she tells me,
as an obvious fact,
we'll be one in death too…..
I have nothing to say
became it is true.

We are one.
She is my conscience too.

She criticizes, in the
way only she can,
completely understanding
and yet giving me
Perspective,
letting me be my best
and ensuring I make no error...

She has made a
Better man of me
than I was
She lets me, giving me space
to be one and in touch always
with my true, real self...

Life is so real, true
simple and hence
beautiful, profound,
grand, deeply joyous with her...

Love can be a
pinnacle and we are that proof...
Oh! My dearest, my only one...
Life is such a blessing,
such a sweet union,
such a completion
because you are me...

We hungrily reach for each other
almost all the time...

Untroubled, calm, serene and
yet violent, ecstatic, tense...

Two souls attracting
like powerful magnets
and never ever reaching
the limit of consummation.

Your kisses, your caresses
transform physicality
into something magical –
A pure state of extreme joy…

We laugh, we look,
in incredible wonder,
it takes time to accept too…

So much happiness is unknown,
seems unreal, yet it is
real, possible, ours, forever…

THE DIVINE THING MINE FOREVER!!

To look at her, at the whole of her, her structure, her soul,
Both together with no separation, and the animated feelings,
Seen clearly to a perceptive mind, to see her walk, talk,
Smil , laugh, think, respond with light in the eyes,
The flow of the body, seen through, her soul and the thing
within,

To love, be struck with that womanly beauty,
To get lost in the dream of the utter beauty in front of you,
To feel that pressure in you, Oh! That delights! To see and to
dream!

And to know that that divine being is yours and you are free
To explore the limits of joy, pure, given to you as a gift!
The wonder of holding and feeling the sharp aching passion,
Possessed by a madness, a human animal, laughing, serene
Yet deeply driven and violent, possessing and tearing apart!
The wonder filled feeling again, the wonder, the pleasure of
life!

Extreme, clearing all rot, cleansing, but simply and laughing!
A yes! yes! yes! to life and living, on and on it goes!

In the deepest union and that is an ecstasy and Pinnacle
reached!!

CONCLUSION

LOVE NEVER DIES.

LOVE CANNOT DIE.

LOVE IS YOU.

LOVE IS LIFE.

LOVE IS THE FULL TRUTH!!

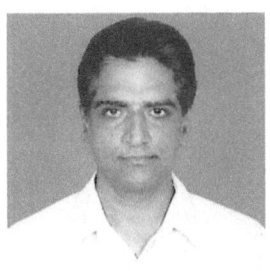

V. Narendra Kumar is a Graduate in B.tech Civil Engineering and MSC (hons) Economics from Birla Institute of Technology and Science, Pilani, India. His prime love is the holistic Nature of Knowledge and he is well versed in both the Physical and Biological Sciences on the one hand and the Social Sciences on the other. He also has a deep understanding of Literature and Philosophy. His mission is to spread the power of knowledge in the whole world. He is well known for his Oratory Skills, Writing Skills and an ability to bring about a deep inner transformation in any student.

Contract:
editornaru@gmail.com
91-8978689120

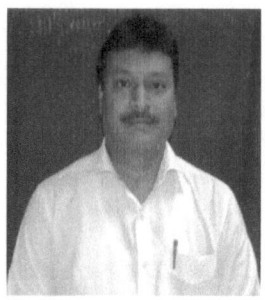

Dr A.C.V. Ramakumar is a Doctorate in Hindi. He has channelized his selfless efforts into developing hundreds of students on the University level. His Mission in life is to spread the power of Education all over the world. He is known for his philosophical depth in Literature, original understanding of all great authors and an ability to reach any kind of student and facilitate inner transformation. Received "The Indian Achievers' award for education excellence", "Best ICT teaching award for education excellence", "Indywood educational excellence award for professional excellence in teaching", "International Academic and Research Excellence Award" and "adarsh vidya saraswati rashtriya puraskar".

EDUCATIONAL WEBSITES: ICT Teaching Methods......
www.thehindiacademy.com
www.nrkacademy.com
www.sonuacademy.in

THANK YOU